Bloomsbury Collection of Modern Art

British Landscape Painting– Nineteenth Century

BLOOMSBURY BOOKS
LONDON

This edition published 1989 by Bloomsbury Books
an imprint of Godfrey Cave Associates Limited
42 Bloomsbury Street, London WC1B 3QJ

ISBN 1 870630 76 9

Printed in Italy by Gruppo Editoriale Fabbri, S.p.A., Milan

The tradition of landscape painting in England has its origins in the seventeenth century, but it was not until the second half of the eighteenth century that it achieved any important results, with the oil paintings of Richard Wilson and Thomas Gainsborough and the watercolors of Paul Sandby, John R. Cozens, and Thomas Girtin. By the end of the eighteenth century, however, the two leading landscape painters, Joseph Mallord William Turner and John Constable, were both in their mid-twenties, and their art was destined to dominate landscape painting for the greater part of the nineteenth century.

J. M. W. Turner

About 1800 Turner had established himself as a painter in both oil and watercolor; he exhibited regularly at the Royal Academy, where he became a member in 1802. At this time his style was essentially eclectic and varied. With his watercolors he had gained some prominence, working in the topographical tradition founded by such artists as Paul Sandby and Edward Dayes. Together with his friend and rival Thomas Girtin (who died at the height of his capabilities in 1802), Turner was developing further in the more romantic manner of Cozens. In his oil paintings, too, Turner reveals various influences, particularly that of the Dutch marine painters and of the classic landscape painting represented by Claude Lorrain and Nicholas Poussin and its continuation in the work of Richard Wilson. In 1802 Turner, taking advantage of the Peace of Amiens to make his first journey abroad, spent about five months in France and Switzerland. This journey awakened in him a lifelong love of Alpine scenes, which is evident in such works as the fine watercolor study *Mer de Glace, Chamonix, with Blair's Hut* (Plate 1), which was done during this journey. Later, Turner used this sketch as the basis for a more detailed watercolor, intended for his patron Walter Fawkes of Farnley, in which the artist's line has become more flowing and his color more brilliant. During his stay in Paris, Turner spent many hours in the Louvre, poring over the works of his great predecessors. In 1803 he showed his first important Claudian composition at the Royal Academy, *The Festival Upon the Opening of the Vintage at Macon* (Plate 2).

The Napoleonic Wars prevented Turner from going abroad again for the next fifteen years, and it was during these years that his depictions of English landscapes reached new heights. About 1807 he produced a series of "pure" landscapes painted directly at the scene, in various spots along the Thames between Walton and Windsor and along the River Wey. In many of these sketches, executed with very free technique, the water constitutes the vital part of the composition; they anticipate by about ten years Constable's naturalistic rendering of the beauties of the English countryside. One of Turner's masterpieces as a painter of the English landscape is *Somer Hill, Tonbridge* (Plate 3).

In the canvas *Snowstorm: Hannibal and His Army Crossing the Alps*, Turner reached the peak of his ability as a painter of dramatic scenes in natural settings. Although the human figures play a clearly secondary role, they nonetheless serve to heighten the fearsome violence of the storm, which rages against the background of a rocky Alpine pass. As in this celebrated composition, Turner felicitously combined landscape and historical subject matter elsewhere in many of his works. A large part of the canvases he exhibited were meant to allude to some historical theme, often indicated in their titles; but this historical content was almost always made wholly subordinate to the landscape element in the painting.

It should be noted, too, that Turner was a master of topographic representation, of rendering nature pure and simple. During the 1820s and 1830s, he did a great deal of work for publishers of landscape engravings, which included several celebrated series such as *The Rivers of France*. The then recently developed method of steel-plate engraving was particularly adapted to reproducing his drawings, and the wide distribution of such engravings that resulted from the new process contributed much to increasing Turner's fame, both in England and on the Continent.

Not until 1819 was Turner able to travel to Italy for the first time. He spent about five months there and visited Turin, Venice, Bologna, Florence, Rome, and Naples. In the course of his travels, he would make hundreds of pencil sketches and thus collect a vast assortment of topographical data. In the following years, Italian landscapes—particularly those of Venice—were among his favorite subjects. As time went on, Turner's drawings from nature became more and more reduced to essentials; only occasionally did he enrich these with touches of color. He undoubtedly was gifted with a remarkable visual memory, which enabled him to re-create seemingly accurate, or at least convincing, color and atmospheric effects months, and even years, after he had visited a particular place.

Between 1820 and 1830 Turner continued to develop toward his more mature style. Toward the end of this period he painted a series of landscapes particularly rich in color and atmospheric effects; these were done at Petworth in Sussex, the seat of his patron, the third Earl of Egremont. A good example of this series is *Petworth Park: Tillington Church in the Distance* (Plate 5). It is evident that the artist felt very much at ease in Petworth, where he had a studio at his disposal. There he was able to realize a more personal style of landscape, in which he blended with great mastery and facility the accumulated experience of his earlier works and the decisive influence of his subsequent travels in Italy.

A natural source of inspiration was Venice, the city of water, which Turner visited at least three or possibly four times: in 1819, 1835, and 1840, and perhaps also in 1832. His first two oil paintings of Venetian subjects appeared in 1833, and with only two exceptions Turner continued to paint Venetian scenes until 1846. The oil entitled *Bridge of Sighs, Ducal Palace and Custom House, Venice: Canaletto Painting* (Plate 8) was one of the first two shown in 1833. Turner's inclusion, in the foreground, of the rather incongruous figure of Canaletto may be interpreted as a sign of respect for his great predecessor as a painter of the Venetian scene. Turner also painted many lovely watercolors of Venetian views, and he continued to use this expressive medium to the end of his life. In the final phase of his career, Turner's oil technique came closer and closer to the brilliant effects he had long achieved in watercolor; in the last ten years of his active life his oil paintings often matched his late watercolors in their luminosity and spontaneity. Turner continued to paint prolifically and worked in both techniques until a few years before his death in 1851. Indeed, one might say that Turner reached the pinnacle of greatness in his art after the age of sixty—an age when most men have passed their creative prime.

The magnificent *Sun Setting over the Sea* (Plate 6), painted about 1845, is in the main an abstract rendering of light and color, a composition in which the only tangible form is the ball of the setting sun. In this, as in many of his late works, Turner reveals the perceptive understanding and love he had long felt for the sea. If it is not always the open sea he deals with, it is water in some form or other that continually recurs in his compositions. This persistent theme is once again expressed in *Norham Castle, Sunrise* (Plate 7), one of the finest of Turner's late works. Here the observer is struck with the beauty of the rising sun, which the artist's brush has captured in a remarkable combination of color and form, revealing a complete mastery of the problems of light posed by the subject. In imaginative and virtuoso paintings such as these, Turner stands out both as the most original of English landscapists and as an inspired romantic artist.

John Constable

Whereas Turner was already an established artist at the beginning of the nineteenth century, his greatest contemporary, John Constable, was barely beginning to make a name for himself at that time. Born at East Bergholt in Suffolk, the son of a prosperous landholder and millowner, Constable had passed his early adult years preparing to enter his father's business. Nevertheless, he had begun to dedicate whatever time he could spare from business affairs to his pencil and paintbrush, already developing that familiarity with and love for the gentle beauties of the Suffolk landscape that was to form the decisive element in his art. His first steps toward artistic creation, however, were unsteady and not very promising; and even when the young Constable was finally permitted to dedicate himself wholeheartedly to the study of painting, his progress continued to be slow.

The paintings of Claude Lorrain and Gainsborough had significant influence on the youthful Constable. Concerning the former, whose work he first saw in *Landscape with Hagar and the Angel*, a fine small canvas then owned by Sir George Beaumont (now in the National Gallery in London), Constable stated that "he was the most perfect landscape painter the world ever saw." About the latter, Constable wrote to a friend, "I fancy I see Gainsborough in every hedge and hollow tree." The influence of both is evident in Constable's first important landscape, a view of Dedham Valley painted in 1802. Its composition echoes Lorrain's small painting mentioned above, and in execution it has qualities in common with the works of Gainsborough in his middle years. Above all, this work reflects Constable's strong determination, and he expressed this in a letter written from London to his friend and fellow artist John Dunthorne, a few months before he returned to East Bergholt to begin work on the painting in question. "However one's mind may be elevated," he wrote, "and kept up to what is excellent, by the works of the Great Masters—still Nature is the fountain's head, the source from whence all originality must spring—and should an artist continue his practice without referring to nature he must soon form a *manner*....I shall shortly return to Bergholt where I shall make some laborious studies from nature—and shall endeavour to get a pure and unaffected representation of the scenes that may employ me with respect to colour particularly and anything else."

During the next ten years Constable studied in detail every possible feature and nuance of the countryside around East Bergholt, particularly the Stour River valley, with its adjoining locks and canals and the mills belonging to his own family. He filled numerous sketchbooks with small pencil studies and also did many spontaneous oil sketches, such as *Near Stoke-by-Nayland* (Plate 10), which effectively reproduces the peculiar light and atmosphere of the scene. In these years Constable rarely went to other parts of England, except for a journey to the Lake District in 1806. Throughout his life he never crossed the English Channel and, moreover, never traveled to any extent within the British Isles. In the Stour Valley, where he had found his first inspiration as a child, Constable seemed to find everything he needed for his masterful and mature accomplishments as a landscape painter.

Boatbuilding near Flatford Hill (Plate 15), shown at the Royal Academy in 1815, was painted in its entirety out-of-doors during the summer and autumn of 1814. Before starting it, Constable had studied once again the works of Claude Lorrain; in this canvas, too, he made every effort to follow the advice of Joseph Farington to "carry his finishing far enough." This painting is notable also because it was the first of Constable's landscapes to include people. By then he had mastered every detail of nature in the Stour Valley, and he now began a series of paintings in which he inserted some narrative content. All of these were based on his intimate acquaintance with life and work along the banks of the Stour. In 1819 he showed the first of his great series of large "six-foot" canal views. These subjects constituted his major output during the next six years. The celebrated *Hay Wain* (Plate 12), the third of this series, was first shown publicly in 1821; it is the only one in the group of six views of the river in which no barge is present. The narrative element in this sun-drenched landscape is provided by the empty haywagon slowly fording the stream under the watchful eye of a dog standing on the near shore.

After a long courtship and engagement, Constable married Maria Bicknell in 1816; thereafter he spent much more of his time in London and only went to East Bergholt occasionally. He now began to look for landscape subjects farther from home. While on his honeymoon, for instance, he made some excellent drawings of the Dorset coast. In 1819, because of his wife's poor health, he took a house in Hampstead, from which he himself clearly derived much advantage, for in the paintings done in those years there are frequent scenes of this hilly district north of London. *Hampstead Heath* (Plate 14) is typical of such views in which the sky always plays a prominent part. It was in Hampstead that Constable began his closer studies of sky, which at first still included a segment of the scenery below. In 1822 he began a series of cloud studies, both in oils and in watercolor, for which he generally made careful notes, writing on the back of his sketch various details regarding the date, the hour of day, and the local weather conditions.

Another significant source of inspiration for Constable in the 1820s was Salisbury Cathedral and its parklike surroundings. He went often to Salisbury to visit the bishop, an uncle of his close friend Archdeacon Fisher, who had been granted a house within the cathedral close in 1819. The graceful forms of the cathedral, with its tall, slender spire, furnished Constable with the central motif of many sketches and paintings. The fine oil sketch of *Salisbury Cathedral and Archdeacon Fishers's House from the River* (Plate 9) is an early example.

Constable had a constant struggle to win public recognition during this phase in his career, and it was not until 1829 that he was accepted for full membership in the Royal Academy. His election to the Royal Academy, when it eventually came, occurred at a most unfortunate time, for his wife had died only a few months before, and he never completely recovered from the tragedy.

Still, Constable continued to paint and found renewed inspiration in the scenery of his beloved Stour Valley. In 1828 he painted *The Vale of Dedham* (Plate 11), another version of the subject he had painted early in his career, in 1802, while under the strong influence of the work of Claude Lorrain. The later version achieves an atmospheric sense of natural light and color with far greater success. Exhibited in 1835, *The Valley Farm: Willy Lott's House* (Plate 16) is the last—and the major—representation of this theme. During his last years Constable began painting his studies from nature mostly in tempera or watercolor, although there are some magnificent oil sketches connected with *The Valley Farm*. These late watercolors and drawings present Constable's most immediate and concise renderings of his vision of the Stour. This vision was not as successful in oils. His last large canvases, such as *On the Stour* (Washington, Phillips Collection), are almost as direct in execution as the later bold drawings, but their tremulous light and restless surfaces make them more difficult to comprehend as total compositions. Though past sixty, Constable still continued to experiment with the oil medium. In 1837, soon after he died, Constable was hailed as England's greatest natural landscape painter.

The Norwich School

For reasons of chronology, it has been advisable to consider the works of Turner and Constable at the very beginning of this study. While their achievements undoubtedly constitute the finest English landscape painting of the nineteenth century, there are many other British artists of this genre and era who merit attention. Among these is the important group forming the nucleus of the so-called Norwich School, which was very active during the first three decades of the nineteenth century. At the beginning of the nineteenth century, Norwich was the chief commercial center of eastern England; indeed, Norwich, then at the peak of its prosperity, claimed to be England's second biggest city. Norwich society, closed and exclusive, was composed of a number of prosperous and cultured families who were patrons of the local artists and also furnished a substantial number of pupils for those artists willing to devote part of their time to instruction in drawing. Although the Norwich painters did not formulate any distinct aesthetic theory, their works were fairly homogenous in style.

The founder of the Norwich School was John Crome, a self-taught painter who received his only training in the arts as an apprentice to a carriage and sign painter. He also had the opportunity to copy the works of such masters as Gainsborough, Hobbema, and Richard Wilson in the house of Thomas Harvey, one of Norwich's major art collectors. Nothing is known of Crome's early work but in his fine composition *Slate Quarries* (Plate 18), one of his earliest surviving works (probably painted about 1802–1805), the influence of Wilson, as well as that of various seventeenth-century Dutch painters, is clearly evident.

Although he had visited the Lake District and Wales in the early 1800s, Crome found his true inspiration in the immediate vicinity of his native city, Norwich. Within the city itself, he painted the tranquil river zone; in the nearby countryside, rolling landscape and secluded dells provided his subject matter. Crome's intensely personal glimpse of the vistas around Norwich is revealed in the large canvas *Marlingford Grove* (Plate 19), very likely painted in 1815. He often painted this peaceful woodland path, with its great variety of trees and shrubs. This interest in and love of trees is clearly seen in many paintings of his mature period. In the last years of his life (he died in 1821, still a vigorously creative painter), Crome often sought inspiration along the seashores of eastern England, whose distinctive light and atmosphere he captured with great vividness and clarity.

Early in 1803 Crome founded the Norwich Society of Artists, which soon became a focal point for local artists, both professional and amateur. The society held its first exhibit in 1805 and continued, almost uninterruptedly, to hold annual exhibitions until 1839. A few of Crome's pupils, including his son John Berney Crome, became prominent members of the society. Among them were James Stark and George Vincent, who closely followed the style of their master, although in their later years they developed a more distinctive manner of their own. Stark's *The Path in the Forest* (Plate 17) can be regarded as typical of the work of these minor members of the Norwich School. Although he was born in Norwich and an active member of the Norwich Society of Artists, John Sell Cotman stands apart from others of the Norwich School and is considered the most gifted artist of them all. Cotman received his training in London; his early works, mostly watercolors, are studies made during his travels in various parts of England. He was particularly impressed by the natural beauties of Yorkshire, which he visited in 1803, 1804, and 1805. There and in the neighboring county of Durham, he painted some of the finest watercolors ever made by an English artist. At first influenced by Thomas Girtin and Turner, his style soon developed a very personal character, especially in his use of line and color. Cotman's solid draftsmanship and mastery of subtly graded color are effectively illustrated in a watercolor entitled *Gretna Bridge* (Plate 20).

At the end of 1806 Cotman returned to Norwich and opened a drawing school, but this venture did not prosper; nor did his own work meet with great favor among the Norwich patrons, who preferred and acquired the more traditional paintings and drawings of Crome and his pupils. Cotman began painting more in oil but still was unable to find purchasers. In fact, his artistic activity was to a great extent disrupted by unceasing efforts to sell his work and increase his income by teaching. Little by little, this lack of success affected his art; his watercolors became harder and more stylized, but the strength and quality of his draftsmanship remained on the whole unaffected.

For his one loyal client, Dawson Turner, a Yarmouth banker and amateur archaeologist, Cotman made a great number of topographic and architectural drawings, many of which were etched as illustrations for Turner's antiquarian writings. One of these works, *The Architectural Antiquities of Normandy*, was published in 1822, with ninety-seven illustrations by Cotman.

From the later 1820s until his death in 1842, Cotman worked largely in oils and painted several genuine masterpieces, usually of small dimensions, such as *The Baggage Wagon* (Plate 21). This painting reveals the concise, sturdy compositional sense and lively handling of paint that were the distinguishing marks of his late works.

The Dutch and Classical Traditions

Until now we have discussed, for the most part, those landscape painters who had gone significantly beyond or purposefully broken with eighteenth-century tradition. It should be kept in mind, however, that other of their contemporaries still looked more to the past for inspiration. One such was Thomas Barker of Bath, the leading member of a family of painters. After a stay in Rome in the 1790s, he spent the rest of his long life in Bath, where he painted genre and historical subjects, as well as landscapes. *Landscape near Bath* (Plate 22), painted in the early years of the nineteenth century, is typical of his meditative landscapes and reveals Barker's substantial debt to his great predecessor Gainsborough.

Like Barker, the Scottish painter Patrick Nasmyth came from a family of artists: his father was a painter, and a brother and six sisters were interested in art. But it was Patrick Nasmyth who was the most gifted artist among this proficient family. His *A Woodsman's Cottage* (Plate 23), dated 1825, is a good example of his essentially Dutch landscape manner—a style that earned him the nickname the "British Hobbema."

The influence of Dutch (and Flemish) art is evident in the work of many nineteenth-century English landscapists, among them James Ward. Although he was primarily a painter of animal subjects, Ward did a number of landscapes that strongly recall the work of Rubens. Nonetheless, in his large-scale and impressive canvas *Gordale Scar, Yorkshire* (Plate 24), a scene first shown publicly in 1815, he achieved a romantic grandeur that was very much his own.

The classical landscape tradition also persisted in the work of certain English artists during the first half of the nineteenth century. Noteworthy among the painters who followed this long-established path was John Glover, who worked both in oils and in watercolor. His technique was meticulous in the extreme (even to the point of using a brush divided into separate segments), but he possessed a strong compositional sense, as seen in his *Borrowdale* (Plate 26), one of the many works inspired by the scenic Lake District. Glover had a considerable but rather short-lived success; by the time he emigrated to Australia, his fairly prosaic traditionalism no longer enjoyed wide popularity.

John Martin then became the leading practitioner of the classical manner in landscape, but in a style very different from Glover's. Martin exhibited huge canvases peopled with minute figures that were overwhelmed by spectacular scenery, landscape and architectural. Although primarily a painter of historical subjects, he had a fondness for a kind of narrative landscape of grandiose proportions. Typifying this form is his *Macbeth* (Plate 27), a smaller version of an immense canvas exhibited in 1820.

The Watercolorists

We now turn to a number of artists who were beginning their careers around 1800 and who contributed greatly to the development of the English Watercolor School. The first of these is John Varley, who in 1804 helped to found the Old Water-Colour Society, which soon became a gathering place for London water-colorists. Varley was also well known as a teacher and several of his pupils became artists of note. His style developed from the manner of Thomas Girtin to a romantic and picturesque style, which was formal and on occasion ponderous and rigid. His colors, while subtle and harmonious, tended to be flat. In later years he evolved a freer technique, though still rather mannered. He found many of his subjects in the mountainous landscape of Wales and was especially interested in effects obtained by contrasting areas of brilliant light with deep shadow. The glowing *Dolgelly, Wales* (Plate 32), dated 1811, exemplifies Varley's early style at its best.

David Cox, who was born in and worked mainly in Birmingham, was five years younger than Varley and was his pupil in 1804, which thus accounts for the strong Girtin influence evident in his early work. Soon, however, Cox developed a vigorous style of his own. He excelled at depicting scenes of turbulence and vigorous movement, as seen in his intense renderings of stormy landscapes, such as *Sunshine, Wind and Rain* (Plate 30), dated 1845; yet he could also capture with great success the quieter aspects of English landscape. He traveled widely in search of inspiration and went to the Continent several times, but Wales remained one of his favorite regions. When he was over fifty years old, Cox began to paint in oils; his achievements in his new medium were remarkable, especially in the superb marine landscapes for which he was celebrated. *Sandy Shore of Rhyl* (Plate 31), dated 1854-55, is an example of these.

Peter de Wint, of Dutch parentage but born in England, was only a few months younger than Cox and, like him, contributed much to English watercolor painting. Unlike Cox, however, De Wint had scant success during his lifetime. Despite this lack of recognition by his contemporaries, generations of English watercolor painters are indebted to De Wint's accomplishments, both in style and in technique. Although his oils are rather pedantic and overly elaborate, De Wint's watercolors are notable for their spontaneity and loose flowing composition. Initially somewhat monotonous in color, his watercolors after 1820 show increasing mastery of the medium. De Wint preferred tranquil scenes such as that of *Harvesttime* (Plate 29), which captures convincingly the shimmering atmosphere of a hot summer's day. In the years between 1840 and 1849, De Wint's watercolor technique reached a masterful peak. One of the finest of his works from this late period is the lovely and tranquil *View near Oxford* (Plate 28).

Another pupil of John Varley was Anthony Vandyke Copley Fielding (who, one might add, eventually lived up to the name given him by his hopeful parents), one of the most renowned English watercolorists in the first half of the nineteenth century, and also one of the very few who achieved financial security through his artistic output. A large part of his work consisted of marine views painted, as were his landscapes, in a deft but perhaps overly facile and superficial style. His landscapes, generally cast in the classical mold, are typified by *Loch Lomond* (Plate 33).

Richard Parkes Bonington

An important influence in the evolution of nineteenth-century English painting was the short but spectacular career of Richard Parkes Bonington, born in England but a resident in France from the age of fifteen until his premature death at twenty-six. At age twenty-two, Bonington exhibited five paintings (four oils and a watercolor) at the Paris Salon of 1824 and, like his noted co-exhibitor John Constable, was awarded a gold medal. During the next four—and last—years of his life, Bonington continued to develop his fresh and highly original landscape style, and he produced numerous paintings and drawings of architectural subjects. He found special inspiration in life along the seashore; a fine example of these seaside landscapes is the well-known *Fisherfolk on the Normandy Coast* (Plate 35), marked by rich color and extraordinary rendering of natural light. In 1826 Bonington went to Italy, where, like Turner, he was especially inspired by Venice—its scintillating combination of reflecting waters, brilliant sunlight or mist, and unique atmosphere. The sketch entitled *Landscape with Mountains* (Plate 34) was painted during this Italian journey, but it is not possible to identify the specific locale. Bonington's palette, both in oils and in watercolor, was exceptionally clear and brilliant; when shown in group exhibitions, his paintings must undoubtedly have stood out from those of his colleagues.

The Topographic Tradition

Roberts and Holland were strongly influenced by the work of Samuel Prout, creator of a watercolor genre of architectural views in which notable or picturesque buildings and monuments were minutely detailed. Prout, who was official watercolor painter to King George IV and Queen Victoria, traveled extensively on the Continent and was especially fond of depicting Gothic architecture. Characteristic of his enormously popular, much-imitated work is the large watercolor *Porch of Ratisbon Cathedral* (Plate 37).

James Holland, in addition to being an excellent draftsman, was gifted with a refined color sense put to best use in Venetian scenes such as *Venice, Rialto Bridge* (Plate 36). When he worked in oils, Holland's style seems to lack spontaneity and become more rigid, and his color more monotonous; these characteristics are also evident in his larger, more ostentatious watercolors, which are sometimes labored and lack the immediacy and brilliance of his smaller sketches.

Much of the same criticism could be applied to the works of David Roberts, which even in his more pretentious efforts, however, did not lack atmospheric pictorial effects. Having studied theatrical design, Roberts shows a flair for the dramatic in his often bold compositions, as can be seen in such Middle Eastern scenes as *The Pyramids of Gîza, near Ancient Cairo* (Plate 38), dated 1845.

The first efforts in draftsmanship by the art critic John Ruskin were pencil sketches copied from works of Prout and Roberts. Although he was an admirer of Turner, Ruskin's feeling for detailed and precise rendering was closer to the style of Prout and Roberts. This kinship is evident in his delicate pen-and-wash sketch, *Piazza delle Erbe, Verona* (Plate 42), dating from 1841. Ruskin's later drawings became even more detailed, but from time to time he abandoned his painstaking studies of monuments for informal sketches of landscape from nature.

James Baker Pyne, born in Bristol, lived in London during the second half of his life and traveled extensively on the Continent in search of subject matter. His landscapes retain much of the classical tradition, such as his delightful view of *Clifton from the Meadows of Ashton Fields* (Plate 40), dated 1836. His color, pale and muted in his earlier Italian scenes, gradually became even more pallid in his late works. Like his master, Pyne's best-known pupil, William James Müller, was fundamentally a classicist, particularly in his large compositions; but unlike Pyne, he preferred strong, darker, and more vibrant color both in oils and watercolor. This preference, already evident in early work such as his *View of Bristol Cathedral* (Plate 41), painted in 1835, became even more pronounced after Müller's travels on the Continent and in the Middle East. His Egyptian and other Middle Eastern scenes brought him a wide reputation and numerous commissions. Many fine, rapid landscapes sketched in the years just before his death in his early thirties are interesting for their appealing color, though their draftsmanship and composition are often weak.

Another artist who traveled widely was Edward Lear, perhaps better known as a writer of humorous verse than as a painter. In his travels, which took him as far east as India and Ceylon, Lear was rarely without his sketchbook, in which he drew in a highly individual style delightful landscapes now much sought after by collectors. Lear himself attached greater importance to his large oil paintings; these, however, tend to be heavy and rigid and lack the exquisitely subtle color sense evident in his watercolors. *The Cedars of Lebanon* (Plate 39), dated 1858, is a fine example of his sure draftsmanship and lovely, delicate tints.

Pastoral Landscapes

While Lear found inspiration for his works in the distant landscapes of Italy, Greece, and the Middle East, many of his fellow artists were content to depict the natural beauties of the British Isles in rustic and pastoral scenes with figures, which often had a narrative element. Typical of these is John Linnell, who studied under Varley and was for some years active as a portrait painter. In middle life he began to devote his time to landscape painting, in which he affected a naturalistic and sentimental manner. Linnell favored harvest scenes and other rustic subjects, such as *The Flock* (Plate 46), painted in 1863.

Similar to Linnell's work in spirit were the landscapes of Richard Redgrave, who is better known for his genre paintings. *"The Valleys also stand thick with Corn"* (Plate 45), painted by Redgrave two years after *The Flock,* is typical of the highly colored, naturalistic and sentimental landscapes that were immensely popular in the mid-Victorian era.

Another painter who satisfied the demand for this type of painting was George Vicat Cole, whose meticulously painted landscapes, almost photographic in their attention to detail, are typified by *Harvesttime* (Plate 44), dated 1860. Vicat Cole developed a successful landscape formula—from which he rarely departed—of painting a minutely detailed foreground, a middle ground only slightly less precise, and a rather hazy background of sky, all in naturalistic colors.

Many painters in this era found it difficult to escape the powerful influence exercised by the new art of photography; the increasing demand for realism and careful detail in rendering became almost irresistible for a time. One artist who did manage to retain his individualism in the face of this was Thomas Creswick, whose landscapes, although generally realistic and somewhat commonplace, are nevertheless effective in conveying atmosphere and personal feeling. *Summer Afternoon* (Plate 47), painted in 1844, is a case in point. Creswick used a fine brush and very thin paint. Although his compositions tend to be dry and fussy, they display a sound construction that gives them more integrity than the loose, more elaborate panoramas of Linnell and Vicat Cole.

Samuel Palmer

For the greater part of his long career, Samuel Palmer produced watercolor landscapes that have much in common with the popular works of his day and with many of the artists mentioned above. In his early years, however, Palmer made an exceptional contribution to English landscape painting during its most romantic phase—now considered one of the most important aspects of this school. From about 1825, while still in his early twenties, until 1834, Palmer followed a "visionary" style suggested to him by the natural beauties of Shoreham, a small village on the River Darent in Kent. In this peaceful, fertile valley Palmer felt the magic of nature intensely and expressed it in vigorous form, with great freshness and delicately detailed rendering, as in his *Pastoral with Horse Chestnut Tree* (Plate 43), dating from 1831 or 1832. By 1835, however, Palmer's delicate touch and poetic sense had begun to decline, and not even in Italy, where he went on his wedding trip in 1837, was he able to recapture these lovely qualities of his visionary early style. He remained abroad to paint until 1839. Although they still have vigor and rich color, Palmer's works of this later period lack the charming spontaneity, sensitivity, and originality of the Shoreham paintings. When he returned to England, he thereafter sought to align himself with the newer trends of the day; but the resulting works were often self-consciously literary in conception and overly elaborate and strained in their execution.

Pre-Raphaelite Influence

Some of the artists who followed the Pre-Raphaelites, or at least were strongly influenced by them, also painted landscapes, adhering to the cardinal precept of that movement—"truth to nature." Notable among these painters was William Dyce, in whose narrative works landscape is often an important element. (His *Gethsemane*, in the Liverpool Museum, is an example.) One of Dyce's masterpieces of "pure" landscape is *Pegwell Bay, Kent* (Plate 48), done in 1859; although painted with great meticulousness, this scene has both strength and a certain spontaneous charm in its contrast of active and statically posed figures.

The same detailed accuracy, but with far less spontaneity, characterizes the work of John William Inchbold, who was regarded as the leading landscape painter of the Pre-Raphaelite Brotherhood and who received much encouragement from John Ruskin. An interesting example of his work is *Landscape: Spring* (Plate 51).

Another artist who earned the support of Ruskin was John Brett, whose *Glacier of Rosenlauen* (Plate 49) shows the influence of Ruskin's aesthetic in its painstaking attention to detail. It was the first landscape exhibited by the artist in 1857. Brett's most famous early landscape, *The Valley of Aosta*, was painted under the direct guidance of Ruskin, who later acquired the work. In Brett's later paintings his intense preoccupation with scrupulous rendering of the most minute elements of landscape led to a stilted, labored style; most of these coastal and marine landscapes, overburdened with detail, are unconvincing and lack compositional unity.

The same faulty compositional structure is evident in the work of Benjamin Williams Leader, who was probably the most popular English landscape painter of the latter half of the nineteenth century, as well as one of the most prolific. His *February, the Ditch Filler* (Plate 50)—still one of the most popular paintings in the City Museum and Art Gallery of Birmingham, England—suffers from this overelaboration of detail and, as a result, does not convey an authentic impression of nature. Technically, Leader was unquestionably an accomplished painter, especially in manipulating color; as a creative artist, however, he lacked subtlety and imagination, and thus achieved little more than photographic naturalism. In his works, color is used as a sort of overtint, rather than as a truly pictorial means.

The English Impressionists

Leader and other artists of similar tendency were oblivious of the important developments then taking place in French landscape painting within the Impressionist circle; then, little by little, this French influence began making itself felt in England. One of the first to abandon the detailed naturalism of Pre-Raphaelite painting and its followers for the new style was Henry Moore, who combined broad, almost Fauvist brushwork and vivid color in his many seascapes. *Arran* (Plate 55), painted at the peak of his artistic powers, shortly before his death in 1894, is a fine example of his style.

The Scottish painter William MacTaggart also had a great love of the sea. Although his paintings have much in common with those of Dutch contemporaries and with the French Impressionists, he is credited with having developed a distinctly personal style, independent of such outside influence. (It should be noted, though, that he did travel on the Continent several times and as a student lived briefly in Paris.) Early in his career, MacTaggart earned his living as a portrait painter; gradually he began painting open-air scenes, in which figures always played a prominent part. Not until the last decade of the century did he begin to concentrate on pure landscape—the coastal views and seascapes for which he is best known. The turbulent, powerful *The Storm* (Plate 54), dating from 1890, is a large canvas painted in the studio from a smaller oil sketch done outdoors at Carradale in 1883. His sun-filled *Harvest at Broomieknowe* (Plate 53) was painted in 1896 in the Midlothian country, where he had settled after leaving Edinburgh some seven years earlier.

James McNeill Whistler

Although born in the United States and trained in France, James Abbott McNeill Whistler belongs more appropriately within the frame of English art history, for the greater part of his active, artistic career was spent in London. From many points of view, Whistler was an enigmatic figure as an artist. Admittedly his works are widely variable in quality, a fact that is particularly noticeable in his landscapes, which often betray the artist's deliberate effort to achieve ever-different and astonishing effects. In such instances, indeed, Ruskin's severe criticism is comprehensible, and even perhaps merited. At their best, however, Whistler's landscapes are marvelously successful in creating convincing atmosphere and evoking lovely poetic moods. His masterful, harmonious blending of qualities deriving from Japanese prints and from the early Impressionist works is apparent in *Valparaiso: Twilight in Pink and Green* (Plate 52), painted during a visit to South America in 1866. In earlier landscapes and coastal views,

Whistler shows a strong artistic debt to Gustave Courbet, whom he met about 1858; later the American artist's style became increasingly abstract in both oils and watercolor, ranging from flat color patterns to suggestive wisps of form created by an almost magical flick of his brush.

Mark Fisher was also born in the United States, and he too spent the greater part of his life in England, painting pastoral landscapes that are fundamentally English in concept and vaguely Impressionist in technique. *On the Road to Newport* (Plate 58), dated 1895, is typical of the fresh, luminous style of his works, painted for the most part out-of-doors from life. Mark Fisher is representative of the English landscape painters of that era who absorbed certain traits of Impressionism but never achieved its magic. In his most successful works, Fisher has been aptly described as "the poor man's Sisley." It should be added that the influence of French Impressionism became more and more evident in England after 1890, when Lucien Pissarro, eldest son of the leading Impressionist artist Camille Pissarro, went to London to live and work.

Philip Wilson Steer and Walter Richard Sickert

Philip Wilson Steer and Walter Richard Sickert were both born in 1860; and they died in 1942, only a few months apart. They are the last two artists to be discussed here, and in their works one sees some of the qualities found in the paintings of the two artists with whom our discussion of landscape art opened —Turner and Constable.

Landscape constitutes the most important part of Steer's output, though he began his career as a figure painter. He studied at the Gloucester School of Art, then in Paris, and exhibited for the first time in London in 1883. His early work reveals the influence of Whistler, and, through this celebrated predecessor, of Japanese art; also apparent is Impressionist influence. During the final decade of the century, however, Steer synthesized these more or less immediate influences and evolved a style more distinctly his own, also experimenting with the styles of such earlier masters as Rubens, Watteau, Gainsborough, Constable, and Turner. In the mid-1890s he returned from his by then familiar coastal scenes with figures to painting the English countryside, particularly views of Yorkshire and Shropshire. In these his palette becomes darker and his application of pigments thicker, as in his 1897 canvas *Richmond, Yorkshire* (Plate 56).

This "dark" phase gave way at the turn of the century to Wilson Steer's most original landscape style, in which he used strong, brilliant color with great freedom and slashing brushwork, as well as with great imagination. The most successful of his paintings of this period, such as *Stroud: Panorama of the Plain* (Plate 57), dating from 1902, were plein-air works painted directly from life, and they reveal the artist's keen perception of atmospheric conditions and the movement of natural light across the landscape. Steer painted similar subjects in watercolor, a medium in which his facility equaled that of Peter de Wint at his best. He continued to produce landscapes of this type until about 1915, after which his work became somewhat stereotyped. He continued to paint until partial blindness put an end to his artistic activity.

As a young man Sickert, like Steer, was markedly influenced by Whistler; in fact, after a brief time at the Slade School, Sickert became the older artist's studio assistant in 1882. The following year, Sickert met Edgar Degas, whose influence was also considerable, especially in the subjects drawn from the theater and cabarets that Sickert began painting in 1887. The drama and vitality of these works carried over into Sickert's landscapes — or more aptly, into the busy urban scenes for which he is remembered. Sickert frankly preferred portraying the bustling activity of a crowded city instead of the quiet pastoral existence of the countryside. He found consistent inspiration in the boulevards and byways of Dieppe, his home in France, and Venice — which he saw for the first time in 1895. In his views of these cities he used a relatively dark, subdued palette; yet, far from being muddy, his paintings gleam with light that emerges from the somber backgrounds to create wonderful atmospheric effects. The carefully detailed *Lion of St. Mark's, Venice* (Plate 59), a work of about 1896, and *Café des Tribunaux, Dieppe* (Plate 60), done in about 1901, furnish good examples of his style in this period. In later works, Sickert's colors are lighter and his brushwork looser; in these, too, his preference for cityscapes over the more conventional bucolic views continued.

Sickert's style exerted a strong influence on some of his fellow artists, who joined him in the "Camden Town Group," founded in 1911. The artists of this group were instrumental in developing a strain of Post-Impressionism that was essentially English in spirit, contributing greatly to a rebirth of landscape painting in England that began with Steer and Sickert.

In examining the work of some forty British painters who, during the nineteenth century, devoted their efforts mainly to landscape, we have noted that this art form reached its peak in the first half of that century and, with the passing of time, lost its earlier impetus and imaginative force. Only on the threshold of the twentieth century did it recover, in the work of Steer and Sickert and others influenced by them, some trace of the genius of their incomparable predecessors Turner and Constable.

PLATES

Joseph Mallord William Turner

PLATE 1   JOSEPH MALLORD WILLIAM TURNER *Mer de Glace, Chamonix, with Blair's Hut,* 1802 (31.5 x 47.5 cm) London, British Museum

PLATE 2 JOSEPH MALLORD WILLIAM TURNER *The Festival upon the Opening of the Vintage at Macon*, 1803 (145 x 233.5 cm) Sheffield, Graves Art Gallery

20

PLATE 3 JOSEPH MALLORD WILLIAM TURNER *Somer Hill, Tonbridge, c.* 1811 (91.5 x 122 cm) Edinburgh, National Gallery of Scotland

PLATE 4 Joseph Mallord William Turner *The Fall of an Avalanche in the Grisons*, 1810 (90 x 120.5 cm) London, Tate Gallery

PLATE 5   JOSEPH MALLORD WILLIAM TURNER *Petworth Park: Tillington Church in the Distance, c.* 1830–31 (65 x 147.5 cm) London, Tate Gallery

PLATE 6   Joseph Mallord William Turner *Sun Setting over the Sea*, c. 1840–45 (91.5 x 122 cm) London, Tate Gallery

PLATE 7 JOSEPH MALLORD WILLIAM TURNER *Norham Castle, Sunrise, c.* 1840–45 (91.5 x 122 cm) London, Tate Gallery

PLATE 8   JOSEPH MALLORD WILLIAM TURNER *Bridge of Sighs, Ducal Palace and Custom House, Venice: Canaletto Painting,*
1833 (51 x 81 cm) London, Tate Gallery

John Constable

PLATE 9   JOHN CONSTABLE *Salisbury Cathedral and Archdeacon Fisher's House from the River,* 1820 (52.7 x 76.8 cm) London, National Gallery

PLATE 10   JOHN CONSTABLE *Near Stoke-by-Nayland, c.* 1807 (35.5 x 44.5 cm) London, Tate Gallery

PLATE 11 JOHN CONSTABLE *The Vale of Dedham,* 1828 (141 x 122 cm) Edinburgh, National Gallery of Scotland

PLATE 12 JOHN CONSTABLE *The Hay Wain,* 1821 (130.5 x 185.5 cm) London, National Gallery

PLATE 13 JOHN CONSTABLE *Study for "The Leaping Horse," c.* 1825 (129.4 x 188 cm) London, Victoria and Albert Museum

PLATE 14 John Constable *Hampstead Heath, c. 1818–19* (54 x 76.9 cm) Cambridge, Fitzwilliam Museum

PLATE 15 JOHN CONSTABLE *Boatbuilding, near Flatford Mill, c.* 1814–15 (50.8 x 61.6 cm) London, Victoria and Albert Museum

PLATE 16   JOHN CONSTABLE *The Valley Farm: Willy Lott's House, c.* 1835 (146 x 124 cm) London, Tate Gallery

The Norwich School

PLATE 17   JAMES STARK *The Path in the Forest* (51 x 76 cm) Norwich, Castle Museum

PLATE 18   JOHN CROME *Slate Quarries, c.* 1802–1805 (124 x 158.7 cm) London, Tate Gallery (Photo: John Webb)

PLATE 19   JOHN CROME *Marlingford Grove, c.* 1815 (136.5 x 100 cm) Port Sunlight, England, Lady Lever Art Gallery

PLATE 20   JOHN SELL COTMAN *Gretna Bridge,* 1805 (24.2 x 33 cm) London, British Museum

PLATE 21   JOHN SELL COTMAN *The Baggage Wagon, c.* 1828 (41 x 35 cm) Norwich, Castle Museum

The Classic and Dutch Traditions

PLATE 22   THOMAS BARKER OF BATH *Landscape, near Bath, c,* 1798 (81 x 106.5 cm) London, Tate Gallery

PLATE 23   Patrick Nasmyth *A Woodman's Cottage*, 1825 (41.5 x 55.9 cm) Edinburgh, National Gallery of Scotland

PLATE 24   JAMES WARD *Gordale Scar, Yorkshire*, 1811–15 (333 x 422 cm) London, Tate Gallery (Photo: John Webb)

PLATE 25   SIR AUGUSTUS WALL CALLCOTT *Dutch Coast Scene, Waiting for the Boats, c.* 1834 (70 x 89 cm) London, Tate Gallery

PLATE 26   JOHN GLOVER *Borrowdale* (41.8 x 60.8 cm) Newcastle-upon-Tyne, Laing Art Gallery

PLATE 27   JOHN MARTIN *Macbeth* (50.8 x 71.1 cm) Edinburgh, National Gallery of Scotland

45

The Watercolorists

PLATE 28   PETER DE WINT *View near Oxford* (29 x 46 cm) London, Victoria and Albert Museum

PLATE 29   PETER DE WINT *Harvesttime* (35.5 x 55 cm) Manchester, City Art Gallery

PLATE 30   DAVID COX *Sunshine, Wind and Rain*, 1845 (46.5 x 60.5 cm) Birmingham, City Museum and Art Gallery

PLATE 31   DAVID COX *Sandy Shore of Rhyl,* 1854–55 (74 x 135 cm) Birmingham, City Museum and Art Gallery

PLATE 32 JOHN VARLEY *Dolgelly, Wales,* 1811 (22 x 48 cm) London, Victoria and Albert Museum

PLATE 33   ANTHONY VANDYKE COPLEY FIELDING *Loch Lomond*, 1884 (25.4 x 35.5 cm) Newcastle-upon-Tyne, Laing Art Gallery

Richard Parkes Bonington

PLATE 34   RICHARD PARKES BONINGTON *Landscape with Mountains* (25 x 33 cm) Edinburgh, National Gallery of Scotland

PLATE 35   RICHARD PARKES BONINGTON *Fisherfolk on the Normandy Coast* (66 x 100.5 cm) Nottingham, Castle Museum and Art Gallery

The Topographical Tradition

PLATE 36   JAMES HOLLAND *Venice, Rialto Bridge,* 1865 (23 x 39 cm) London, Bethnal Green Museum

PLATE 37 SAMUEL PROUT *Porch of Ratisbon Cathedral* (65.4 x 46.3 cm) London, Victoria and Albert Museum

PLATE 38 DAVID ROBERTS *The Pyramids of Giza, near Ancient Cairo*, 1845 (24 x 34.2 cm) London, Victoria and Albert Museum

PLATE 39   EDWARD LEAR *The Cedars of Lebanon*, 1858 (35.5 x 54.5 cm) London, Victoria and Albert Museum

PLATE 40   James Baker Pyne *Clifton from the Meadows of Ashton*, 1836 (84 x 132 cm) Bristol, City Art Gallery

PLATE 41   WILLIAM JAMES MÜLLER *View of Bristol Cathedral*, 1835 (72 x 133 cm) Bristol, City Art Gallery

PLATE 42   JOHN RUSKIN *Piazza delle Erbe, Verona,* 1841 (34 x 48.2 cm) Oxford, Ashmolean Museum

Pastoral Landscapes

PLATE 43   SAMUEL PALMER *Pastoral with Horse Chestnut Tree, c.* 1831–32 (33.9 x 26.7 cm) Oxford, Ashmolean Museum

PLATE 44   GEORGE VICAT COLE *Harvesttime*, 1860 (95.9 x 151.7 cm) Bristol, City Art Gallery

PLATE 45   RICHARD REDGRAVE *"The Valleys also stand thick with Corn,"* 1865 (71 x 97 cm) Birmingham, City Museum and Art Gallery

PLATE 46 JOHN LINNELL *The Flock*, 1863 (71 x 100 cm) Birmingham, City Museum and Art Gallery

PLATE 47 THOMAS CRESWICK *Summer Afternoon*, 1844 (102 x 127 cm) London, Victoria and Albert Museum

65

The Pre-Raphaelite Manner

PLATE 48   WILLIAM DYCE *Pegwell Bay, Kent (A Recollection of October 5, 1858),* 1859–60 (63.5 x 89 cm) London, Tate Gallery
(Photo: John Webb)

PLATE 49   JOHN BRETT *Glacier of Rosenlauen,* 1856 (44.5 x 42 cm) London, Tate Gallery

PLATE 50   BENJAMIN WILLIAM LEADER *February, The Ditch Filler,* 1881 (119.5 x 182 cm) Birmingham, City Museum and Art Gallery

PLATE 51   JOHN WILLIAM INCHBOLD *Landscape: Spring* (51 x 35 cm) Oxford, Ashmolean Museum

The English Impressionists

PLATE 52   JAMES ABBOTT MCNEILL WHISTLER *Valparaiso: Twilight in Pink and Green*, 1866 (58.5 x 75.5 cm) London, Tate Gallery

PLATE 53   WILLIAM McTAGGART *Harvest at Broomieknowe,* 1896 (87.2 x 130.2 cm) Edinburgh, National Gallery of Scotland

PLATE 54   WILLIAM McTaggart *The Storm*, 1890 (120 x 181 cm) Edinburgh, National Gallery of Scotland

PLATE 55   Henry Moore *Arran*, 1894 (30.5 x 54.7 cm) Manchester, City Art Gallery

PLATE 56 PHILIP WILSON STEER *Richmond, Yorkshire,* 1897 (46 x 61 cm) Oxford, Ashmolean Museum

PLATE 57 PHILIP WILSON STEER *Stroud: Panorama of the Plain*, 1902 (56 x 69 cm) Oxford, Ashmolean Museum

PLATE 58   MARK FISHER *On the Road to Newport*, 1895 (75 x 90 cm) Manchester, City Art Gallery

PLATE 59   WALTER RICHARD SICKERT *The Lion of St. Mark's, Venice, c.* 1896 (90 x 90 cm) Cambridge, Fitzwilliam Museum

PLATE 60   WALTER RICHARD SICKERT *Café des Tribunaux, Dieppe, c.* 1890 (60.4 x 73 cm) London, Tate Gallery

THE ARTISTS

THOMAS BARKER of Bath

Born in Pontypool in 1769. Barker gained the patronage of a rich carriage manufacturer, who sent him to Rome to study in 1789–90. Barker returned to England in 1793 and lived for the rest of his life in Bath, where he painted landscapes and scenes of rustic life. He exhibited from time to time at the Royal Academy and the British Institution. He died in Bath in 1847.

RICHARD PARKES BONINGTON

Born in Arnold, near Nottingham, in 1802. When he was fifteen, his family emigrated to Calais, France, where he took lessons from Louis Francia, a watercolor painter. In 1819 Bonington ran away to Paris, armed with an introduction to Delacroix, who was favorably impressed by his work, and in 1820 he entered the studio of Baron Gros. Bonington exhibited for the first time at the Paris Salon of 1822, with a series of his watercolor sketches; in 1823 he traveled through northern France and painted coastal landscapes. Besides his more celebrated landscapes, he also painted historical subjects, mainly episodes in French history. He went to England for a short time in 1825, and in 1826 he traveled in Italy. In Venice he fell ill with tuberculosis and returned to England, where he died in 1828.

JOHN BRETT

Born in Bletchley in 1830. At the age of twenty-three Brett entered the school of the Royal Academy in London. He exhibited for the first time in

BONINGTON *Study for "The Plain of St. Denis, Normandy"*

BONINGTON *Romantic Young Woman*, Besançon, Musée des Arts Décoratifs

1857, and two years later he showed his most famous work, *The Stonecutter* (Liverpool Art Gallery), which brought him the encouragement and friendship of John Ruskin—a friendship that ended a few years later. Brett was elected an associate of the Royal Academy in 1881, but he never became a full member. Brett died in Putney in 1902.

AUGUSTUS WALL CALLCOTT

Born in London in 1779. He began by studying music, but then turned to art and entered the Royal Academy in 1797, also becoming a pupil of John Hoppner. Callcott began his career as a portrait painter, but later he devoted most of his time to landscape and marine painting, for which he found great inspiration in Dutch art. He became an associate of the Royal Academy in 1806 and a full member in 1810. In 1827 he journeyed to Italy, and in 1837 he was knighted in recognition of his considerable artistic reputation. He died in London in 1884.

GEORGE VICAT COLE

Born in Portsmouth in 1833. Vicat Cole worked in his father's studio and first exhibited in 1852. He became an associate of the Royal Academy in 1870 and a full member ten years later. Specializing in views of the Thames Valley and Surrey, he devoted himself completely to landscape painting. He died in London in 1893.

JOHN CONSTABLE

Born in East Bergholt, Suffolk, in 1776. Constable at first planned to join his father's firm, but in 1799 he enrolled in art classes at the Royal Academy in London. He exhibited for the first time in 1802, devoting himself fully to landscape painting. From then on he divided his time between London and his native Suffolk, occasionally visiting other parts of England.

In 1816 Constable married Mary Bicknell. In 1819 he was elected an associate of the Royal Academy. He exhibited at the Paris Salon of 1824. In 1829 he became a full member of the Royal Academy and published a series of mezzotints the following year in the first issue of *English Landscape Scenery*.

Constable's landscape painting, so much admired by later generations, brought him little recognition among his fellow Englishmen during his lifetime. He died in London in 1837.

JOHN SELL COTMAN

Born in Norwich in 1782. At the age of sixteen, Cotman went to London to study painting and exhibited at the Royal Academy from 1800 to 1806. During these years he traveled extensively, and on his return to Norwich he became a leading member of the Norwich Society of Artists and opened a drawing school there. In 1812 he moved to Yarmouth and later spent some time in Normandy (1817–20). He returned to Norwich in 1823 and remained there until 1834, when he was appointed professor of drawing at King's College in London. He died in London in 1842.

CONSTABLE *Group of Trees, Landscape and Study of Clouds* (27.5 x 36.2 cm) Florence, Museo Horne

COTMAN *Portrait of His Father, John Sell Cotman,* London, British Museum, Reeve Collection

DAVID COX

Born in a Birmingham suburb in 1783. Cox began his career as an itinerant scene painter and then, in 1804, went to London to study with the painter John Varley. He exhibited at the Royal Academy in 1805. In 1813 he joined the Old Water-Colour Society, where he showed his work regularly. In 1813 and 1814, while teaching art himself, he published *A Treatise on Landscape Painting and Effect in Water-Colours*. About 1840 Cox settled in Harborne, near Birmingham, and began painting in oils, but his watercolors remain his most admired achievement. He died in Birmingham in 1859.

THOMAS CRESWICK

Born in Sheffield in 1811. Creswick studied in Birmingham under J. Vincent Barker and settled in London in 1828. He was elected an associate of the Royal Academy in 1842 and a full member in 1851. A prolific artist, he also did many book illustrations. In his later years Creswick painted mainly in oil, finding his preferred subjects in the countryside and streams of north England and Wales. He died in Bayswater in 1869.

GORDON *Portrait of David Cox*, Birmingham, City Art Gallery

JOHN CROME

Born in Norwich in 1768. Crome was apprenticed at an early age to a sign and house painter, and he spent his leisure time sketching from nature. In 1790 he met Thomas Harvey of Catton, the wealthy owner of a large collection of paintings by Dutch and English masters, who allowed Crome to copy works from his collection and later helped him to become a drawing master.

Crome rarely left his native Norfolk but made, in 1814, an ambitious jaunt to Paris and Belgium for the purpose of seeing a collection of artworks confiscated by Napoleon. In 1803 he helped found the Norwich Society of Artists (of which he became president in 1808) and thereafter showed annually at the group's exhibits. His work was shown at the Royal Academy between 1806 and 1818. He also produced some fine etchings (*Norfolk Picturesque Scenery*, 1834).

Crome, who died in Norwich in 1821, is familiarly known as "Old Crome" to distinguish him from his son, John Bernay Crome (1794–1842).

PETER DE WINT

Born at Stone, in Staffordshire, in 1784. De Wint was sent to London in 1802 to be apprenticed to the engraver and portrait-artist John Raphael Smith. Later, he studied with John Varley and, in 1809, became an associate of the Royal Academy. From 1810 on he was a member of the Old Water-Colour Society, where he showed most of his work. De Wint traveled extensively in the British Isles but went abroad only once, to Normandy in 1828. For most of his life, he was a drawing master. De Wint died in London in 1849.

WILLIAM DYCE

Born in Aberdeen, Scotland, in 1806. Dyce was compelled by his family to study medicine and theology; secretly, however, he devoted his leisure time to painting. About 1824 he abandoned his other academic studies to enter the Royal Scottish Academy in Edinburgh and then the school of the Royal Academy in London. He visited Italy twice, in 1825 and 1827–28. In Rome he was much impressed by the Italian Primitive School and entered into close association with the German Nazarene painters. In 1830 he settled in Edinburgh and became an associate of the Royal Scottish Academy. In 1838 he moved to London and in 1840 was appointed secretary of the newly organized Government School of Design at Somerset House. He was made an associate of the Royal Academy in 1844 and a full member in 1848. Also in 1844, he became a professor of fine arts at King's College. He collaborated on the fresco decoration of the House of Lords (*Baptism of Ethelbert; King Arthur*). Dyce died at Streatham, in Surrey, in 1864.

ANTHONY VANDYKE COPLEY FIELDING

Born at Halifax, in Yorkshire, in 1787. Fielding studied under John Varley and later married Varley's sister-in-law. He became a member of the Old Water-Colour Society about 1810 and was elected its president in 1831. A rapid and prolific worker, Fielding produced great numbers of somewhat facile landscape and marine subjects and reputedly earned a large fortune from their sale. He died in 1855 in Worthing.

MARK FISHER

Born in Boston, Massachusetts, in 1841. Fisher first studied with the painter George Inness and then, in 1861, went to Paris to study with the Swiss painter Charles Gleyre. He returned to the United States but then, finding little opportunity for commissions there, settled in England in 1872. He became a member of the New English Art Club, was elected an associate of the Royal Academy in 1911, and a full member in 1919. He died in London in 1923.

JOHN GLOVER

Born at Houghton-on-the-Hill in 1767. Glover was entirely self-taught. After a time as a successful teacher of drawing and painting in Lichfield, Staffordshire, he moved to London in 1805 and exhibited at the Old Water-Colour Society, of which he was later elected president twice. Earlier, in 1795, he had shown his work at the Royal Academy. In 1831 he emigrated to Australia, where he continued to paint and teach. He died in Launceston, in Tasmania, in 1849.

JAMES HOLLAND

Born at Burslem, in Staffordshire, in 1800. As a boy Holland worked as a china painter, specializing in floral decorations. In 1819 he moved to London, where he continued to paint flower pieces. After a stay in Paris in 1831, he turned to landscape painting and soon acquired prominence in this field. Holland traveled widely on the Continent and exhibited frequently at the British Institution, the Society of British Artists, and the Old Water-Colour Society. He died in London in 1870.

JOHN WILLIAM INCHBOLD

Born in Leeds in 1830. In 1847 Inchbold entered the school of the Royal Academy in London, where he exhibited for the first time in 1851. He was strongly influenced by the early work of the Pre-Raphaelites and earned praise from John Ruskin. Inchbold's later painting was very uneven in quality, perhaps because he was depressed by a reversal of fortune and was tormented by financial difficulties. He died in Leeds, impoverished, in 1888.

BENJAMIN WILLIAMS LEADER

Born in Worcester in 1831. In 1853 he entered the school of the Royal Academy, where he showed his work for the first time in 1854. He began as a painter of rustic genre, but, after settling in 1862 in Whittington, near Worcester, he became increasingly interested in landscape. He became an associate of the Royal Academy in 1883 and a full member in 1898. He died in Shere, in Surrey, in 1923.

EDWARD LEAR

Born in London in 1812. At the age of fifteen, Lear began painting birds and animals. Between 1832 and 1836, he was commissioned by the thirteenth Earl of Derby to depict the birds in his menagerie at Knowsley, in Lancashire; afterward, Lear wrote his first *Book of Nonsense* (1846) for the earl's grandson. In 1836 he turned to landscape painting.

MARSTRAND *Portrait of Edward Lear*, 1840, London, National Portrait Gallery

He spent much time abroad and lived for nearly ten years in Rome. From 1850 to 1873 he exhibited regularly at the Royal Academy. Widely acclaimed as a painter and illustrator in his own time, Lear is even better known today for his delightful nonsense books and clever limericks. He died in San Remo, Italy, in 1888.

JOHN LINNELL

Born in London in 1792. Linnell studied with John Varley and entered the school of the Royal Academy in 1805. From 1818 on, he was a close friend and patron of William Blake and, in turn, was much influenced by that artist. At first he was active mainly as a painter of portraits and miniatures, but in 1847 he began to paint landscapes. He also did some engraving. He showed regularly at the Royal Academy from 1807 to 1881, but was consistently rejected for membership. Linnell died at Redhill, in Surrey, in 1882.

JOHN MARTIN

Born at Haydon Bridge, near Hexham in Northumberland, in 1789. As a youth Martin studied with the Italian painter Bonifacio Musso and then, in 1806, moved to London, where he worked for a time as a heraldic and glass painter. He began showing his paintings at the Royal Academy in 1812; in 1816 he won attention with his *Joshua*

Commanding the Sun to Stand Still.

Martin also illustrated books. Less popular — but perhaps his best works — are the dramatic, small landscapes he painted and later used for background details in his crowded, grandiose historical scenes. He died at Douglas, on the Isle of Man, in 1854.

WILLIAM MacTAGGART

Born at Kintyre, in Argyll, Scotland, in 1835. MacTaggart studied in Edinburgh and at the Trustee's Academy in Glasgow, where he specialized in portraiture. He then painted genre scenes in the Pre-Raphaelite manner and did not turn to landscape until 1880–90. He became an associate of the Royal Academy in 1859 and a full member in 1870. About 1890 he moved from Edinburgh to Broomieknowe, where he died in 1910.

HENRY MOORE

Born in York in 1831. He learned to paint from his father and later studied for a short time at the Royal Academy School (1853). Moore's early work shows strong Pre-Raphaelite influence; subsequently, he was inspired by French Impressionism. Shortly before 1860, he began painting mainly marine subjects. In 1885 Moore became an associate and in 1893 a full member of the Royal Academy. He died at Margate, in Kent, in 1895.

WILLIAM JOHN MÜLLER

Born in Bristol in 1812. Müller studied painting with J. B. Pyne. In 1831–38 he traveled extensively, and after settling in London in 1839, he joined an archaeological expedition to Lycia in 1843. He returned to England in 1844 in poor health and died the following year in his native Bristol.

PATRICK NASMYTH

Born in Edinburgh in 1787. Nasmyth studied with his father, the painter Alexander Nasmyth (1758–1840), before settling in London in 1810. Throughout his career he painted landscapes in the Dutch manner. Nasmyth showed regularly at the Royal Academy, the British Institution, and the Society of British Artists, of which he became a member in 1823. He died in London in 1831. (Referred to as the "British Hobbema" in his day, he is sometimes known as Peter Nasmyth.)

SAMUEL PALMER

Born in London in 1805. Palmer exhibited at the Royal Academy for the first time at the age of fourteen. He was essentially self-taught. In 1824 he met William Blake, who became a strong influence on Palmer. Between 1827 and 1835 he lived in Shoreham, a small village in Kent; during this time, his so-called Shoreham period, he produced paintings of great originality.

In 1837 Palmer married Linnell's daughter and went to Italy, where he remained to study and paint for two years. On his return to England he gradually abandoned oils for watercolors. He

PALMER *Three Oak Trees and a Beech Tree: Lullingstone Park,* 1829 (29.5 x 47 cm) London, Miss Hilda Pryor Collection

joined the Old Water-Colour Society in 1843 and exhibited thereafter in their group shows. He later turned to etching. He died at Reigate, in Surrey, in 1881.

SAMUEL PROUT

Born in Plymouth, in Devon, in 1783. Prout studied under a local drawing master and began to work at an early age as a topographical draftsman. He specialized in minutely detailed drawings of picturesque architecture and landscapes, showing a preference for the Gothic style. He traveled widely in the British Isles and on the Continent, and in 1803 he exhibited at the Royal Academy.

Prout was appointed watercolorist to King George IV and later to Queen Victoria. From 1815 on, he exhibited frequently at the Old Water-Colour Society, of which he became a member in 1819. He died in Camberwell, London, in 1852.

JAMES BAKER PYNE

Born in Bristol in 1800. He abandoned a legal education to study painting and was largely self-taught.

His productions included both oils and watercolors. He moved to London in 1835. He traveled in Italy and other European countries to research and find new subject matter, specializing in river and lake scenes. Pyne died in London in 1870.

PROUT *Mt. Aventine*

RICHARD REDGRAVE

Born in London in 1804. Redgrave exhibited at the

Royal Academy School in 1825 and attended courses there the following year. His genre and pastoral paintings, mostly in oils, were popular with critics and public alike. Elected an associate of the Royal Academy in 1840, he became a full member in 1851. In 1854 Redgrave was appointed

ROBERTS *Málaga: Frontispiece of the "Landscape Annual"*

inspector-general of the Royal School of Design, as well as Keeper of the Crown Collection of Paintings, of which he compiled the first catalog. He died in London in 1888.

DAVID ROBERTS

Born in Edinburgh in 1796. Roberts began his artistic career as a scene painter and designer for the theater in Edinburgh and Glasgow. In 1822 he moved to London, where he worked at Drury Lane Theatre. By then he had begun painting landscapes and architectural subjects in oils and in watercolor and, in 1824, became one of the founding members of the Society of British Artists.

Roberts traveled extensively in Europe and in Egypt and Syria, where he found the subject matter that was to inspire his painting for the next ten years. In 1851 he spent time in Italy. In 1838 he was elected an associate and in 1841 a full member of the Royal Academy. He died in London in 1864.

JOHN RUSKIN

Born in London in 1819. Ruskin had already studied drawing with Copley Fielding and J. D. Harding when he entered Oxford in 1836. In the summer of 1841 he went on a sketching tour to Italy, where he made many of the finely detailed drawings and watercolors he continued producing for the rest of his life.

Ruskin is perhaps better known, however, as an art critic. An ardent champion of such artists as Turner and the Pre-Raphaelites, he was a powerful and influential figure in the art world of the latter half of the nineteenth century. He also did etchings for books. Throughout his life he wrote prolifically on art and, after 1860, wrote extensively on economic, political, and social problems. He lectured widely and was appointed Slade Professor of Fine Art at Oxford University, a post he held twice (1870–79, 1883–84). In 1871 he founded and endowed the Ruskin School of Drawing at Oxford.

After 1878 Ruskin was afflicted with recurring attacks of brain fever, and in last years he rarely left Brantwood, his house at Coniston, in the Lake District, where he died in 1900.

WALTER RICHARD SICKERT

Born in Munich, Germany, in 1860. His family settled in England in 1868. He was an actor for a few years, but in 1881 he entered the Slade School of Art, where his work came to the attention of Whistler. Sickert left the school the following year to become Whistler's studio assistant, and during this time he traveled regularly to Paris, where he met Degas in 1883. In 1893 Sickert opened an art school in Chelsea and, in 1899, he settled in Dieppe.

RUSKIN *Pine Trees in Sestri, Gulf of Genoa*

SICKERT *Interior with a Figure*, formerly in the collection of C. Maresco Pearce, Esq.

He returned to London in 1905 and became one of the leading figures of the famed "Camden Town period," which became the Camden Town Group in 1911 and later became the London Group. Sickert became an associate of the Royal Academy in 1924 and a full member in 1934; he resigned a year later, however, in a spectacular row with the directorate. After World War I he returned to Dieppe but settled again in London in 1922.

Sickert was one of the few modern artists to use the work of studio assistants in his paintings, in the manner of Renaissance masters. A prolific writer also, he was given to expressing highly controversial opinions. He died in Bath in 1942.

JAMES STARK

Born in Norwich in 1794. Stark became a pupil of John Crome in 1811, at first following the latter's artistic manner, but later evolving a highly individual mode of expression. He showed for the first time at the Norwich Society exhibition of 1809; in 1814 he went to London to study at the Royal Academy School. He returned to Norwich in 1819, resuming his active membership in the society, and he remained in his native town until 1830, when he went back to London. In 1840 he settled in Windsor. He died in London in 1859.

PHILIP WILSON STEER

Born at Birkenhead, in Cheshire, in 1860. Steer studied at the Gloucester School of Art and in Paris at the Académie Julian and the École des Beaux-Arts.

From 1884 on, he spent winters in London and the summers painting in rural England and in France. He exhibited Impressionist-influenced canvases at the Royal Academy from 1883 to 1886 and at the Grosvenor Gallery. His first one-man show was held at the Goupil Gallery in 1894. Steer was a founding member of the New English Art Club and in 1893 was appointed professor of drawing at the Slade School, a post he held until 1930. He was awarded the Order of Merit in 1931. He died in London in 1942.

JOSEPH MALLORD WILLIAM TURNER

Born at Covent Garden, London, in 1775. After studying with Thomas Malton, Turner entered the school of the Royal Academy in 1789 and exhibited there for the first time in 1791. He became an associate of the Royal Academy in 1799 and a full member in 1802—one of the youngest ever.

After years of collaboration with Thomas Girtin, Turner did his first oil paintings in 1796 and 1797. He was greatly influenced by the works of Richard Wilson and Claude Lorrain. In 1802 Turner made his first trip abroad, to France and Switzerland. In 1807 he published the first volume of his *Liber studiorum*, an ambitious work on landscape painting, and that same year he was appointed professor of perspective at the Royal Academy.

After 1816 he continued to travel to the Continent. He was elected vice-president of the Royal Academy in 1845. He died in Chelsea in 1851.

Turner *Devil's Bridge*, London, National Gallery

Orpen *Tribute to Manet* (from left to right: G. Moore, W. Steer, H. Tonks, H. Lane; standing: D. S. McColl, W. Sickert), Manchester, City Art Gallery

JOHN VARLEY

Born in Hackney in 1778. Varley was first apprenticed to a silversmith, but he began to study drawing in 1794. In 1798 Varley exhibited for the first time at the Royal Academy (a drawing, *View of Peterborough Cathedral*). In 1804 he was one of the founding members of the Old Water-Colour Society, and over the years Varley himself showed more than seven hundred works in the group's exhibitions. He was also a teacher; among his pupils were many of the best artists of that period, including Cox, De Wint, Fielding, Linnell, and Palmer. He wrote on the subject of perspective and was also an inventor. Varley died in London in 1842.

JAMES WARD

Born in London in 1769. Apprenticed in his youth to the engraver John Raphael Smith, Ward had turned to painting on his own by 1787. Imitating the work of George Morland (who later became his brother-in-law), Ward at first specialized in animal paintings and rustic scenes. In 1794 he was appointed painter and mezzotint engraver to the

Prince of Wales; in 1800 he was commissioned by Josiah Boydell to do two hundred paintings of various breeds of livestock. This project was never completed, however, because Boydell went bankrupt.

Ward was elected an associate of the Royal Academy in 1808 and a full member in 1811. During the last twenty-five years of his life Ward's health, artistic ability, and fortunes declined. He died at Cheshunt, in Hertfordshire, in 1859.

JAMES ABBOTT McNEILL WHISTLER

Born in Lowell, Massachusetts, in 1834. As a child, Whistler lived for several years in Russia. In 1851 he entered West Point Military Academy, but was dismissed in 1854 for failing examinations. He then worked as a coastal survey cartographer and from this assignment he learned to etch.

In 1855 Whistler went to Paris and studied art. In Paris he met Fantin-Latour, Courbet, and later the Impressionists, who would affect his own art appreciably. In Paris, too, he attempted compositions in the Japanese manner. During this period he exhibited at the Salon des Refusés.

About 1860 he settled in London. In the same year he exhibited for the first time at the Royal Academy; his last appearance under Academy auspices was in 1872, with the celebrated *Portrait of the Artist's Mother: An Arrangement in Gray and Black* (No. 1). Displeased by the cool reception given his works, he turned to one-man shows, the first of which occurred in 1874.

In 1879 he went to Venice to make a series of etchings, in an effort to alleviate his financial situation. Successful in this, he then returned to London to live in Chelsea, where his salon be-

TURNER *Self-Portrait when Young, c.* 1798 (75 x 59 cm) London, Tate Gallery

came a fashionable gathering place for artistic and literary figures. He died in London in 1903.

TURNER *Morpeth, Northumberland*

List of Illustrations